For Your Garden

SHADE GARDENS

~ For Your Garden ~
SHADE GARDENS

WARREN SCHULTZ

Little, Brown and Company
Boston   New York   Toronto   London

MT BS DP EM OD HT HB ES RP AD AB SG EJ CADCC

First Edition

ISBN 0-316-77598-3

Library of Congress Catalog Card Number 94-75707

A FRIEDMAN GROUP BOOK

10 9 8 7 6 5 4 3 2 1

Published simultaneously in Canada by Little, Brown & Company (Canada) Limited

FOR YOUR GARDEN: SHADE GARDENS
was prepared and produced by
Michael Friedman Publishing Group, Inc.
15 West 26th Street
New York, New York 10010

Editor: Kelly Matthews
Art Directors: Jeff Batzli and Lynne Yeamans
Layout: Philip Travisano
Photography Editor: Susan Mettler
Production Associate: Camille Lee

Color separations by Fine Arts Repro House Co., Ltd.
Printed and bound in China by Leefung-Asco Printers Ltd.

Table of Contents

INTRODUCTION

*S*hade. The very word sends chills through most gardeners. To many, shade is synonymous with gloom and bleakness and is often perceived as perilous to garden plants. A lack of sun, however, doesn't have to be a handicap in a garden. In fact, with the wide variety of plants and plethora of designs that are well suited to life in minimal light, it's time to look at shade with a positive attitude.

In the landscape, shade creates a natural time-out. It beckons passersby to stop and rest, making it an ideal spot to place benches and tables. Meandering paths winding through shadows invite a stroll in cool relief from the hot summer sun. Shade also casts an air of mystery as it obscures and blurs and softens hard edges. Certainly, a world without shade would be a desolate and unforgiving place.

Shade is not monolithic, however; it is shrouded in subtleties. Whether it is light, medium, or dark or dappled or fleeting, the wise gardener is glad for a bit of shade and will learn how to use it in the landscape.

ABOVE: A shady spot can become an important feature in the garden, allowing the designer to focus attention on favorite plants. Here, a wise combination of foliage plants offers a variety of cool green colors and different shapes and textures to provide interest throughout three seasons.

OPPOSITE: Wherever you find a stately tree gracing an expansive front yard, you'll find dignified shade as well. Old, tall trees cast a high, dappled shade that's easy to work with. This type of gentle half-shade is ideal for many flowering and foliage plants. Even a finicky lawn thrives under it.

ABOVE: Shade, of course, creates an oasis, a welcome escape from the pounding sun. Out of direct sunlight, this patio is a delightful place to sit and relax and sip iced tea on a hot summer afternoon. The soft white blooms scattered throughout the window boxes and pots accentuate the coolness of the shade.

RIGHT: A shade garden can be wild and naturalistic—as well as brightly colored. With just a little push of the imagination, a woodland setting can be improved with a generous planting of azaleas. Traveling this woodland path evokes the feeling of being submerged in a sea of blooms.

OPPOSITE: A vivid splash of color can add a natural punctuation point to a woodland floor in early spring. With the help of some carefully placed *Narcissus cyclamineus* planted in a casual pattern, this tranquil scene comes alive. Serving to anchor the yellow blooms, a winter currant bush, rarely seen in North American gardens, is dotted with red flowers.

ABOVE: Shade is often the impetus for creating a striking landscape feature. Rather than struggle with growing turf in the shade cast by a wall, this gardener has planted a bountiful bed of impatiens. Abundant with bright blossoms, these mounding plants are perfect for beds, and they'll gladly grow up against buildings where grass won't survive.

ABOVE: Foliage plants rule in the shady border, but just because they lack conspicuous flowers certainly doesn't mean they have to be dull. Here, eye-catching caladiums virtually shout for attention and allow for no mistaking where the path leads.

OPPOSITE: Some trees, such as this old apple, cast only light shade, and their shadows interfere very little with the growing process of the plants around them. In many cases, it's even possible to grow a lawn right up to their trunks.

ABOVE: Shade isn't always an uncontrollable product of nature. Sometimes a small man-made patch of shade can be created for visual interest and to permit the gardener to grow certain plants. This porcelain berry vine shades the window box below, keeping the hot, drying sun from the impatiens.

OPPOSITE: Shade often makes strange bedfellows. The moderate, shifting light of dappled shade allows for combinations not seen in full sun or deep shade. Here, ferns spread in the deepest shade along the trunk of the tree, while primulas and trollius take advantage of the lighter shade along the edge of the bed.

ABOVE: Patio gardens are usually in the shade of a tree or a house, but there are plenty of flowers that sport bright blossoms in less than full sun. Bright begonias are perfect for growing in shaded boxes and pots.

LEFT: Sometimes shade is best left untouched—or seemingly untouched. Visitors strolling down this winding, shady path will be delighted by the single azalea blazing at the bend.

OPPOSITE: Shade can be manufactured or built to suit the gardener. This gazebo provides a shady spot for relaxing among the plants, while also permitting enough light to pass through for plantings to thrive beside it. Even roses bloom vigorously in the dappled light.

Chapter One

GRADES OF SHADE

The face of shade can be as changeable as the weather, and like snowflakes, no two spots of shade are the same. In fact, the degree of shade in a single area of the garden may change from season to season, from day to day, and even from hour to hour. The quality of shade is also determined by what is casting it. A wall or fence will cast a denser shade than a tree or bush. Even the height, type, and age of a tree will make a difference.

However, if forced to squeeze shade into categories, it can be labeled either light, medium, or deep. Light shade is cast by tall trees, medium shade is created by densely branched trees or shrubs, and deep shade is caused by evergreens and buildings. There are plenty of flowers that will welcome a place in light shade, blooming profusely once there. Medium shade often offers enough light for some flowering plants, but this is where foliage plants such as hosta shine. Only the heartiest plants will survive in the deep shade, making it an ideal place for ground covers. If you carefully analyze the shade in your own garden, you should be able to find the perfect plants to suit your shade requirements and your garden design.

RIGHT: Shade comes in all grades and degrees. Many levels are often present in a single garden as such shade-loving plants as azaleas and rhododendrons create an even heavier layer of shade beneath them. In the understory, interest can be provided by foliage plants. Here, the combination of light and dark shade and undulating levels of glacial outcroppings provide surprises around every turn.

OPPOSITE: High, dappled shade is often the state of affairs in wooded, natural landscapes. The sun isn't completely blocked out but peeks in and out through the trees during the day, so that underplantings such as this foamflower will receive enough sunlight to thrive.

19

ABOVE: Layers of trees and a substantial brick wall make for different grades of shade. In the foreground, where the shade is lighter, a white-flowering shrub provides a bright break. Farther back, tucked into the deep shade of the wall, are foliage plants.

OPPOSITE: Even the most heavily shaded area can have a silver lining. Try breaking up the gloom with selective plantings. Here, a path through a heavily wooded area is accented with tiny wildflowers.

ABOVE: In most yards, there are usually a few spots where the shade is deep enough to create lawn problems. Instead of trying to resuscitate brown turf, take advantage of medium shade by digging out the lawn and replacing it with vibrant flowering beds.

ABOVE: Medium shade, including dappled light from trees, creates a perfect setting for a patio. Offering respite from the sun, the trees shadowing this brick patio let in enough light for flowering potted plants.

ABOVE: Pots brimming with flowers will introduce a jolt of color to a shaded area. Here, begonias are right at home in shallow dishes surrounding the trunk of a tree. Although sunlight falls freely on the garden in the background and the foreground is completely in shade, the sun reaches beneath the tree in early morning and late afternoon, providing enough light for blooming plants. These begonias will bloom happily in the moderate shade provided.

OPPOSITE: Arbors can be used to create light shade and combine two distinctly different types of plants. Here, the sun-loving *Laburnum* thrives as it dangles from the arbor. At the same time, the *Allium giganteum* below receive just enough light shade to keep them fresh and long blooming.

ABOVE: Many gardeners would be amazed at the variety of flowering plants that will bloom quite happily in light shade. In fact, shade can be used to provide relief for sun-loving plants. Here, these apothecary roses won't need as much water during the hot summer months because the ground will stay cooler and moister protected by this canopy of shade at midday.

ABOVE: As shade moves across a garden throughout the day, the dimmer light will cause bright-colored flowers, such as these nasturtiums, to appear deeper in hue. Light shade will also save these blooms from fading too quickly: Note how those flowers on the left already appear to need some relief from the blazing sun.

Chapter Two

MAKING THE MOST OF SHADE

Once you've learned to recognize the changing faces of shade, the next step is to figure out how to make the most of it. When planning the garden, think of the benefits of shade and the mood it evokes, and then plan and plant to enhance and work with a shade-filled area, taking advantage of the shade instead of fighting against it.

Offering cool relief, shade provides an ideal environment for a quiet stroll or a peaceful stopping place for relaxation. Paths, for example, are a natural addition to a heavily canopied section of the landscape, while benches and small pools or ponds

are the perfect garden embellishments to accent the beckoning and comforting nature of shade. You can incorporate luxurious foliage plants into the setting and interplant them with vibrant annuals that will bloom all summer or perennials that will offer splashes of cheery color. Once you start working with the shade instead of railing against it, you'll be amazed at the options that present themselves.

ABOVE: Ah, the allure of shade. The promise of respite from the sun draws visitors to this rustic wooden bench. The white rhododendrons provide a soothing naturalistic backdrop and encourage a longer stay.

OPPOSITE: A worn stone bench is a natural accoutrement for the deep, deep shade of this setting. Cool and dark like the shade itself, the bench seems almost alive with its color and texture matching the rhododendron and trillium leaves.

ABOVE: Sometimes it is best to give in to shade, taking a cue from its shape and form. Here, a path traces the shade as it winds through the woods. Hosta gracefully edges the woodchip trail, providing a beautiful transition between what is man-made and what is natural.

OPPOSITE: Rather than clearing trees to create an expanse of lawn, this landscape plan took only as much of the woods as needed for an intimate patio. Nestled into a glade of shade, this natural setting has preserved the feeling of living at the edge of a cool woodland. Shade-loving azaleas are appealing in this environment, because even when they are not in bloom, their shiny, waxy foliage is attractive.

ABOVE: No matter where this sun-dappled path leads, its tunnel-like appearance is inviting and irresistible. The light shade cast by the heavily wooded landscape creates an ideal growing environment for this mountain laurel arbor, which wouldn't survive in the direct sun.

OPPOSITE: Shaded passageways and stepping stones seem to be meant for each other. Here, violas grow profusely between field-stones, softening the edges of the walk. It's tempting to stroll bare-foot through this garden, feeling the cool comfort of the stones on your feet.

ABOVE: Medium shade is a classic location for a tranquil garden pool, with many bog and water plants preferring this type of muted light. The water reflects the silhouettes of the overhanging trees, which create a layered, deeper shade.

ABOVE: Living with shade casts it in new light. As you become familiar with your conditions and investigate, study, and monitor your shade, you will discover how you can manipulate the shadows to suit your garden style and design. Here, high-branched trees create shade at midday when the sun is directly overhead but allow in enough light early and late in the day to let a colorful woodland garden flourish. It is also possible to remove some lower tree branches to create sunnier conditions.

RIGHT: A reflecting pool is often the solution to a deep-shade dilemma. It provides visual interest in a spot where perhaps nothing will grow, and the reflection creates the illusion that the area is chock-full of color.

ABOVE: Ground covers make a wonderful lawn substitute in low light conditions. Creating a luscious sea of verdant foliage around a tree, this pachysandra will stay green throughout most of the year and will require virtually no maintenance. A ring of red impatiens cleverly breaks up the color scheme, taking further advantage of the shade.

ABOVE: Pots work wonders in the shade. They can be planted with species such as this *Nicotiana thakham* that will flourish in dim light, or as long as the pots and the plants in them aren't too big, they can be planted with sun-loving species and moved around the garden periodically to capture some rays. In this way, surprising blooms can grace even the darkest spot.

ABOVE: Statuary can be used to brighten a shady spot and add visual interest to predominant foliage. Here, it seems natural to encounter this figure resting for a moment in the shade. It's where we would choose to stop if time permitted.

OPPOSITE: While containers can bring color to dim corners, shade returns the favor. Out of the glare of the sun, plants in pots require less water and care. Here, marguerites and white verbena make fine companions in this urn.

Chapter Three

GROUND COVERS AND FOLIAGE PLANTS

*W*hen standing face-to-face with shade, think green. Foliage plants or ground covers are good choices for the backbone of a shade garden design. The absence of flowers, however, doesn't mean that the beds have to be dull. Ferns, for example, bring the exotic touch of the tropics to a garden, while ivy evokes the ambience of a venerable British estate.

Foliage plants and ground covers combine beautifully with each other and with flowering plants, and there is no shortage of shades, textures, and forms available. Ground covers are certain to grow and spread even in the heaviest of shade; in light shade, they can provide a background or frame for brighter plants.

OPPOSITE: If a large patch of ground cover appears too monotonous, it can be broken up with statuary, hardscape, or landscape features that don't rely on sunshine to bring out its beauty. Here, an elegant statue is spotlighted in a field of pachysandra.

ABOVE: English ivy is the classic, foolproof creeping foliage plant for the shade. There seems to be no nook or cranny too dim for ivy. It creeps, it crawls, it climbs in all but the very darkest of areas. You can cut it, tromp on it, and otherwise mistreat it and ivy will still keep on growing. And through it all, ivy carries a stately, aristocratic air.

ABOVE: Adding a splash of color in medium shade, blue star creeper is a delicate species best used to cover small areas. The small-leaved, low-growing plant is covered with tiny, bright blue flowers from spring into summer.

OPPOSITE: A neatly edged bed of confederate jasmine presents a formal look in this less-than-sunny spot. Easily trimmed with shears or a lawn edger, ground covers can be kept in bounds and shaped to suit any surrounding.

ABOVE: Shady ground covers don't have to be restricted to ground level. Here, *Lamium* creeps along a stone wall, adding a second dimension to the garden and providing unexpected fresh color and texture to an otherwise straightforward retaining wall.

ABOVE: A very vigorous grower, gout weed earns its name. It spreads like wildfire in sunny locations but is much better behaved in shady spots. Here's a good example where shade can be used to control the growth of a plant. This extremely hardy, deciduous perennial is favored mainly for its beautifully variegated cream and green foliage.

ABOVE: Some plants seem to be made for each other as well as for the shade. This artful, fail-safe combination of ferns, hostas, violets, and *Lamium* 'Beacon Silver' includes varying heights, textures, and hues to add depth to a shady spot.

RIGHT: Some gardeners plant trees just for the sake of creating shade to grow hosta. Formerly called funkia and found only in basic green, hosta can be found today in hundreds of varieties that range from green to gold to yellow and come in variegated combinations of them all. Most send up long stalks of small, often fragrant flowers in midsummer.

ABOVE: Hosta are perfect plants to place along a shady walk. Their full, clumplike growth pattern softens the edges of a path and provides lush foliage to tickle the ankles. The plant thrives in medium to heavy shade and loose soil.

ABOVE: Shade is an especially welcome commodity in the heat and humidity found in the southeastern United States. Warm-region gardeners have the option of growing palms and ginger to provide rich, tall foliage as a backdrop to ferns, a favorite where the living is easy.

OPPOSITE: For a touch of the exotic to brighten that patch of sun-deprived landscape, look no further than the ostrich fern. It brings a tropical, junglelike feeling to any garden.

Chapter Four

SHORT-TERM SHADE SOLUTIONS

SHADE-LOVING ANNUALS

Gardeners often think of annuals as bright faces for sunny spots, but it's surprising how many annual flowers and vines shine in the shade. Begonias, coleus, and impatiens, among others, will grow fast and take advantage of the changing circumstances throughout the growing season. In addition, annuals are versatile and mobile and can be used to alleviate problem spots in the landscape. They're especially well suited for containers and can provide a vibrant focal point when added to pots, hanging baskets, and window boxes. Many annuals can be started from seed at home. Plan to plant them closely in the shade to take full advantage of their color and form.

RIGHT: Sometimes nothing but color will do—even in the shade. The choices may be limited, but as long as there are impatiens, there can always be color in the garden. In addition to their bright, eye-catching hues, impatiens are also treasured for their growing speed and flexibility. Even under trees or against walls, they grow so fast that they provide almost instant, ground-hiding color.

OPPOSITE: Available in a variety of colors, perky, bushy impatiens grow quickly in the shade to form drifts of everblooming plants. Designs and hues can be changed from year to year or even month to month to provide the best show.

ABOVE: Not a monolithic blanket of dimness, shade is often a very individualized combination of light and dark. The shade on this front porch is dappled with shifting light that's ideal for hanging baskets, window boxes, and pots filled with foliage plants, Boston ivy, and impatiens.

ABOVE: The splashy, variegated leaves of coleus present a colorful twist to this otherwise traditional shade garden. The coleus is a surprising contrast to the classic, bright orange New Guinea impatiens hugging the trunk of the small tree.

ABOVE: Ferns fit nicely into any shady nook. Hardy perennials, they provide a reliable background for annual color. Here, flowering tobacco is tucked in among the fronds, growing amazingly well in light to medium shade and sporting a fine crop of beautiful blossoms. Many cultivars of flowering tobacco are also extremely fragrant, especially in the evening, which will extend the allure of the shady spot into the night.

ABOVE: With huge, rich-colored blooms, tuberous begonias provide incomparable color for shady window boxes, pots, baskets, and beds. If started early in spring, the tubers will quickly grow to provide attractive foliage as well as color throughout the summer.

RIGHT: Shining in this semishady cottage garden, these showy biennial foxgloves will bloom the first season if started early indoors, much like annuals. Although often listed as sun-loving, foxgloves grow well in semishade, their colors even more vibrant out of the bright sun.

ABOVE: Wildflowers can also range into the shade. This packaged mix of thickly sown meadow flowers snuggles up to a tree, creating the illusion of a small meadow bursting with blooms in this flower-filled backyard.

OPPOSITE: The light shade cast by high-branched trees creates some interesting possibilities. Here, shade-loving ivy nestles up against a gleaming ice plant, known primarily as a sun lover. It will bloom profusely, however, in light shade, and although it's a perennial in this California garden, it must be treated as an annual in cooler climates.

Chapter Five

PERMANENT SHADE SOLUTIONS

SHADE-LOVING PERENNIALS

*S*hade grows deeper and expands over the years as shade-casting trees grow taller and more dense, making shade-loving perennials a good garden bet. Set them in the earth and perennials make themselves at home in the shadows, spreading out as the years pass and making the spot their own.

From astilbe to dicentra to viola, there are plenty of perennials that are made for the shade. With a seemingly limitless gallery of colors, forms, and blooming seasons to choose from, perennials are the way to go when you want to give a sense of permanence to your shade bed.

ABOVE: Azaleas make a spectacular statement in the shade. Native woodland plants, they don't pine for sunshine but bloom their best in dappled light. They can be planted closely together to create a hedge of color in early to midspring. The hardy bushes can be left to grow at will or trimmed to control their shape and size.

OPPOSITE: Azaleas can create quite an impact when sprinkled throughout a woodland garden. Planted as specimens, they are a pleasure to stumble upon while strolling along a woodland path. Azaleas are fast and easy growers provided they are planted in slightly acidic soil.

ABOVE: In addition to color, shape and texture create a memorable effect in the shade. Here, the hedge in the foreground has been sculpted to present azaleas at their best. Although the flowering plants represent only a fraction of the plantings here, they present more of an impact because of the artful trimming.

ABOVE: Rhododendrons explode with huge, popcorn-ball blooms early in spring. They seem to shine from within and brighten the shadows around them. Here, in medium shade, the bushy plants pair nicely with the ground-hugging trillium below.

OPPOSITE: A vigorous bloomer in shade throughout the summer, feathery astilbe can be paired with other shady bloomers for maximum effect. Here, planted in combination with astilbe, primulas show off their delicate pastel blooms by shooting them forth like fireworks on slender stems above low, prostrate foliage. The hosta in the right corner provides a broad-leaved exclamation point, and it too will bloom later in the season.

ABOVE: Flaring like tongues of pastel flame, astilbe blossoms bring cheer to the shade. A popular shade-loving herbaceous perennial, this species is well loved for its soft, soothing colors and ferny foliage.

ABOVE: With its intense yellow and orange flowers, the cowslip primrose is a common sight in meadows and along roadsides in Europe. Shown here in a garden in the United States, the plants make wonderful partners for Virginia bluebells. Both are at their floriferous best in spring.

OPPOSITE: The pendulous blooms of bleeding heart dangle abundantly in early spring in all but the darkest shade. When the flowers appear, each shaped like a perfect little heart, it becomes clear where the plant's name came from. The foliage is also attractive, although it usually dies back in the heat of summer. In this garden spot, the vibrant ajuga will hide the scanty bleeding heart foliage throughout the summer.

ABOVE: Shady areas are often moist as well, but fortunately there are several perennials that thrive under these conditions. Here, stately *Ligularia* sends up long stalks of bright yellow blooms in midsummer, making a spectacular statement at the edge of a shady walkway and a delightful companion to Matilija poppies and daylilies.

ABOVE: Columbine adds a dainty touch to the shady bed or border. The nodding tubular blooms appear in clear, bright colors of white, red, violet, orange, pink, and more. There are many hybrid varieties that can be easily grown from seed. Very hardy plants, columbines will bloom freely the year after they are sown.

ABOVE: Daylilies are often found in the brightest of places, but don't get the wrong idea about their sun requirements. Sporting a phenomenal range of colors, most daylilies will gladly bloom unabated throughout the season where there is dappled sunshine or half-shade.

RIGHT: Asiatic natives, lilies will provide a naturalistic or woodland look to the landscape, flourishing in the medium shade of an open wood or wooded environment.

OPPOSITE: A relative of the buttercup, anemones thrive in partial shade. There are many species and cultivars, with showy, five-sepaled flowers in red, white, pink, or purple. Some species spread rapidly and can be naturalized in shady meadows.

ABOVE: European wood anemones bloom in the shade early in the spring. The flowers are small and either white or light purple. They're a pretty alternative to spring bulbs in areas that are too shady for tulips or hyacinths.

OPPOSITE: A European native, cyclamen is beginning to make an appearance in North American shade gardens. Although not reliably hardy, cyclamen does do well in warmer climes, producing slightly fragrant red blooms in spring. The foliage is of interest, too, with white etchings along the edges of each leaf.

PHOTO CREDITS

©Philip Beaurline: 6, 9, 31
©Cathy Wilkinson Barash: 8, 22, 30, 34
©Crandall & Crandall Photography: 20, 21, 33, 41, 67
©Derek Fell: 36, 46 bottom, 50, 53, 56, 59, 69 right
©John Glover: 25, 38
©Saxon Holt: 42, 44
©judywhite: 11, 15, 16, 19, 29, 32, 35 top, 46 top, 49, 51, 52, 54, 57, 60, 64, 69 left
©Dency Kane: 7, 18, 58
©Lynn Karlin: 69 left
©Michael Landis: 43
©Robert E. Lyons: 12, 55 top
©Charles Mann: 17 bottom, 21, 23, 24, 26, 27, 37, 45, 47, 55 bottom, 62, 63, 65, 66, 69 right
©Clive Nichols: 2, 13, 14, 39, 48, 68, 71
©Jerry Pavia: 17 top, 40
©Joanne Pavia: 10, 61, 70
©Richard Shiell: 35 bottom